HOW TO MAKE
COFFEE SO GOOD
YOU'LL NEVER WASTE
MONEY ON STARBUCKS AGAIN

Luca Vincenzo

WATERBURY
PUBLISHERS

Cover Designed by: Damon Freeman

Published by: Waterbury Publishers, Inc.

www.waterburypublishers.com

Visit the author's website:

www.makingespresso.com

CONTENTS

BETTER COFFEE FOR LESS MONEY—
WHY YOU SHOULD READ THIS BOOK

IF YOU BOUGHT THIS BOOK, you probably agree with me that coffee is *awesome*. While we may not know what each new day will bring, we know we'll start them off with a delicious, aromatic cup of coffee (or two), and that's always worth getting out of bed for.

But have you ever done the math on how much you spend in coffee shops?

At most chain stores like Starbucks, Caribou Coffee, and The Coffee Bean, a plain old cup of coffee will cost you about $1.75. If you bought a cup every day, that would be $8.75 per week. If you did this every week, it would cost you $35 per month and $245 per year. Pretty expensive, no? If you only buy a few cups per week, that's still around $150 per year.

And that's spending as *little* as possible! If you like fancier drinks, you can double those numbers. Imagine spending $500 per year on just your morning coffee!

Well, I wrote this book to not only save you a couple hundred dollars per year, but to also show you how to make *better* coffee yourself, using inexpensive equipment that you can keep at home or the office.

A regular cup of coffee shouldn't cost you more than about $0.20 to make, and a fancy "-ccino" drink maybe tops out at $0.50. That's an eighth the price of coffee chains—not bad.

Home-brewed coffee also doesn't have to taste like a bitter cup of hot water with a dash of charcoal. It can taste "chocolaty," without any added chocolate. It can have hints of citrus, without ever coming near fruit. It can be something you look forward to every morning for more than a kick of caffeine.

So, if you're ready to learn how to make some of the best coffee you've ever tasted and save some cash too, let's get started!

1

THE BARISTA'S GUIDE TO COFFEE BEANS

FRESH, HIGH-QUALITY COFFEE BEANS are probably the most over-looked aspect of brewing delicious coffee. Inferior beans will always make inferior coffee, regardless of how fancy your machine is or how many brewing tips and tricks you try.

In this chapter, you're going to learn everything you need to know about coffee beans, so you can whip up heavenly cups of coffee every time.

WHAT IS A COFFEE BEAN, ANYWAY?

Coffee beans are the seeds of berries that grow on trees (yep, coffee grows on trees!). There are usually two seeds, or beans, per cherry. Almost all the world's coffee is produced in hot regions, because that's where it does best. Coffee trees need quite a bit of water, shade, and sun, but don't require good soil.

Coffee trees are a part of the plant genus *Coffea*, and there are thousands of species of plants in this genus. These plants vary greatly in size and shape, but only two types are used in producing commercial coffee beans: *Coffea arabica*, and *Coffea canephora*, also known as *Coffea robusta*.

Arabica beans are, without doubt, the better choice for coffee making. They're grown in the Americas as well as parts of Africa and Asia, and their flavors vary depending on where they're grown—some arabicas have a hint of other berries (Ethiopian Harrar is known for a blueberry flavor), some are very earthy (Indian and Indonesian coffees are known for this), while others have a hint of citrus (common with Central American beans). Around 75% of all coffee grown today is arabica.

Robusta beans are harsher in taste and have more caffeine than arabica. Premium robustas are used in espresso blends because they greatly help with producing a smooth, buttery *crema*, and they add a bit of bite to the shot. It's tough to find great robusta beans, however, because most coffee growers focus their efforts on producing high-quality arabicas. Poor-quality robustas are often used in instant coffees, freeze-dried coffees, and coffee-flavored frozen drinks that rely on sugar and cream to hide the horrible, burnt taste of bad robusta beans.

HOW DO YOU TALK ABOUT BEANS?

Coffee connoisseurs often talk about the "complexity," "acidity" and "body" of beans. What are they talking about?

Complexity: This refers to the number of elements in the cup of coffee—aromas, textures, and tastes. Roasters often roast and blend different coffees to achieve a varied profile.

Acidity: Not to be confused with the pH scale of chemical acidity, the coffee term refers to the "refreshing, mouth-cleansing quality, a sparkling, lively taste" that can help you wake up in the morning. This is also referred to as the "brightness" or "liveliness" of a coffee.

Body: The sensation that the coffee elicits from your tongue, whether it feels "heavy", "thick", or "oily."

HOW ARE BEANS PROCESSED?

If beans are "dry processed," it means they have been washed and then laid out to dry in the sun for several weeks. During this process, the pulp ferments and imparts a unique taste to the beans. Weather and temperature also affect the eventual quality and taste of the beans. After the beans are dried, they are put in machines that remove the dried-up, outer layers of the berries and wash the beans.

A "wet-processed" bean is one that comes from a berry that first had its outer-skin removed by machine. Then, the remaining fruit pulp and beans were placed in a tank and allowed to ferment. Natural bacteria and enzymes eat away the pulp and the beans are then washed and dried (either by the sun or in a machine), and then processed in machines to remove the remaining layers.

"Semi-wet processing" is also a method of preparing coffee beans, and it entails removing the outer-skins of the berries and then letting the pulp and beans dry in the sun like in dry processing. The remaining layers are then removed by machine and the beans are washed.

One method of processing isn't necessarily "better" than another—they just produce different-tasting beans. Dry-processed beans are usually heavy in body, sweet, smooth, and complex. Wet-processed beans produce cleaner, brighter, and fruitier coffee. Semi-wet processed beans are known for having a taste that's in between dry- and wet-processed beans: They're usually sweeter than wet-processed beans with a bit of body and acidity.

How beans are processed changes their taste more than anything else. The differences between and wet- and dry-processed Brazilian coffee will usually be more noticeable than two wet-processed coffees from different regions. Therefore, I recommend that you try beans processed in each of the ways to see what best suits your palate. If you want to get fancy, you can blend different types of beans to create your ideal coffee experience (something we'll talk more about soon!).

WHAT TYPES OF BEANS SHOULD YOU BUY?

Don't think that buying arabica beans will ensure you're ready to make great coffee. The label "arabica" is no promise of quality and, in fact, a fair amount of the arabica out there is actually pretty poor.

As taste is a subjective matter, I can't conclusively tell you which types of beans are "best." But I can help you understand what your options are, so you can experiment with them and find what's best for you.

COUNTRY OF ORIGIN

There are over 40 countries that produce and export coffee, and each product is different and ever-changing (coffee berries grow eight or more times per year and no two batches of beans taste the same). Each coffee-growing region has its distinctive characteristics, though, and you should know them.

I want to go over what I think are the best regions to buy coffee from, a great starting point for your coffee-tasting adventures.

JAMAICA

Jamaica is best-known in the coffee world for their Blue Mountain region, which produces quite expensive coffee referred to as (what else) "Jamaican Blue Mountain." Genuine JBM comes from only a handful of approved estates, and the roasting, sale, and export of JBM is strictly regulated by the Jamaican government and the Coffee Industry Board.

So what's all the fuss about? The best lots of JBM beans are known for their mild flavor and lack of bitterness. However, most professional roasters today agree that the taste isn't as good as it was in the 60s and 70s, and the brand now relies more on its prestige and mystique than its quality to justify the sky-high prices.

There's also quite a bit of counterfeit JBM out there, which is clearly evident from the simple fact that the annual sales of "JBM" are always higher than the actual yearly production. If a coffee says it's "Jamaica Blue Mountain style," it has no actual JBM beans in it. If a blend calls itself a "Jamaican Blue Mountain blend," it only needs to contain 5% authentic JBM to make that claim.

Nevertheless, many people swear by JBM and are happy to pay the premium for it. A good alternative to JBM is Jamaican High Mountain coffee, which is grown by estates in the area that aren't approved to label their coffee as JBM. JHM coffees are very good and much cheaper than JBM.

HAWAII

Hawaii is the only US state that grows coffee, although several US territories grow it. Its best-known coffee comes from the district of Kona, which is located on the western coast of the island of Hawaii. Coffee growing in this region goes all the way back to 1829, and many of the trees are over 100 years old.

For coffee beans to bear the stamp of Kona, they must be grown in this region. Kona beans make superb coffee famous for its rich flavor and intense aromas. While not cheap, Kona beans are less expensive than JBM and many people feel their price is more justified.

As with JBM, watch out for Kona imposters. Kona "blends" may contain only small quantities of genuine Kona beans (as little as 10%, which is what's required by law). Look for beans that have a "100% Kona" certificate or a "Kona Coffee Council 100%" seal on the bag—these are the real deal.

All coffee aficionados should try out 100% Kona beans to see if they catch their fancy.

BRAZIL

Brazil is a coffee giant. It's the largest producer of low-quality arabica beans and quite a bit of robusta too. Some espresso blends are 90% Brazilian and these beans are used in most canned coffee and big roasters' blends.

That being said, Brazil also produces delicious, high-quality coffee beans too. Every good espresso blend that I've tasted used a premium Brazil as its base because they produce great crema and body, which is a great foundation for other coffees.

Experience has taught me that the best Brazilian beans come from the Sul de Minas, Mogiana, Cerrado and Matas de Minas regions. Two microregions in Cerrado are of special interest: Chapadao de Ferro and Serra de Salita.

You can't go wrong with a great Brazil, so I recommend you experiment to find what you like most.

GUATEMALA

Guatemalan coffee is world-renowned for offering one of the most flavorful and subtly complex cups you can find.

Coffee from the Antiqua region is probably the most celebrated of all Guatemalan coffees. Coffee from the Hehuetenango region can also be exceptional and full of fruity flavors. Coban, Fraijanes and Quiche are also regions that produce great coffee.

Central American coffees bring a wonderful zing to a blend, which wakes up the palate. Check out not only Guatemalan coffee, but El Salvadoran and Nicaraguan too! As an added little tip, try Bourbon and Pacamara varietals from El Salvador; also, I think the best Nicaraguan coffees come from the Segovia, Jinotega, and Matagalpa regions.

YEMEN

Yemen is a little country below Saudi Arabia that produces some truly wonderful coffee. It's famous in the coffee world for its "Mocha" port, from which it ships its coffee.

Yemen offers one of the most distinct flavors of coffee in the world. Bright and complex, it is alive with notes that range from candied fruit to dark chocolate with a medium-to-full body.

If you want a unique cup of coffee, give Yemen beans a try, but don't blame me if you get addicted!

KENYA

Kenya is an African coffee powerhouse. In general, Kenyan coffee is a bright, complex cup full of interesting fruit flavors (berries and citrus), with an occasional dash of spice.

Despite the political turmoil in the region, Kenya takes its coffee trade very seriously. Their research and development is unparalleled and quality control, meticulous. Many thousands of small farmers are extremely knowledgeable in how to produce top-notch coffee beans, and it shows in the cup.

You'll pay a premium for Kenyan coffee, but it's well worth it. Give it a try—I think you'll agree.

ETHIOPIA

It would be remiss of me to not include Ethiopia in this list as it's not only the birthplace of coffee, but it also produces high-quality beans. The forests of the Kaffa region were the "cradle of coffee civilization," with arabica beans growing in the wild. Slaves taken from these forests spread the beans elsewhere and well, as the saying goes, the rest is history.

The best Ethiopian coffees come from the Sidamo, Yirgascheffe, and Limmu regions. Really great beans such as the dry-processed Koratie are just spectacular in flavor.

WHAT ABOUT BLENDING?

Creating your own unique coffee blends is where the real fun begins. By honing your own house blend, you can create the exact coffee experiences that you desire. There are a few "rules" of blending that will ensure you get the desired results:

1. Brew and taste each of the coffees separately. Record aroma, fragrance, flavor, acidity, body, and aftertaste. Brew and taste coffees next to each other to determine which coffees augment the flavor of another. Remember that blending coffee beans is an art and the goal is that the whole must be greater than the sum of the parts.

2. Start with a base of a sweet and heavy-bodied coffee and add a small amount of another coffee to it (before you brew it, of course!). Understand the flavor profile of your base and understand your goal. Ask yourself what coffees might be added to this base to achieve the cup you want. Note the change when adding this coffee and repeat with other coffee origins.

3. Next, try mixing three or four other coffees together until you get a blend that displays the flavor characteristics you desire.

4. After determining what type of coffee you would like to use in your blend, begin experimenting with different ratios until you have de-

termined the best ratios to bring out the flavor, sweetness, body and aftertaste desired.

5. If you're roasting your own beans, experiment with different roasts of each coffee in the blend in the same manner you experimented when adding other coffees to the base. Roast one coffee a little lighter or darker than the other coffees in the blend and note any differences. It is usually preferable to roast each coffee separately to its own individual peak and then blend coffees to create the most complexity.

2

THE UNSUNG HERO OF COFFEE: THE GRINDER

BUYING A COFFEE GRINDER IS a better choice than using pre-ground coffee. By using your own grinder, your whole-bean coffee will stay fresh longer, and they're fun to use.

Who wants coffee made with stale beans, anyway?

Let's explore the fascinating world of coffee grinders that are on the market today.

TYPES OF GRINDERS

There are two types of coffee grinders: burr grinders and blade grinders.

BURR GRINDERS

Burr grinders use a spinning metal plate to shred the coffee evenly. Most newer machines are automatic, meaning that you program them how much coffee you want and how fine you want the grind to be.

Conical burr grinders are the best type of burr grinder. They preserve the most aroma and their grind is very fine and very consistent. The intricate design of the steel burrs allow a slow grinding speed, which imparts less heat to the ground coffee, thus preserving maximum amount of aroma. The better conical burr grinders can also grind extra fine for the preparation of Turkish coffee.

Several companies now make low-end ($25 and under) burr grinders.

You should stay away from these, as the low-end models often overheat the grounds and do a lousy job of grinding.

If you don't have much money to spend, I think you're better off getting a blade grinder. But a good grinder can make a *big* difference in the quality of your coffee, so you should seriously consider buying a nice one.

BLADE GRINDERS

Blade grinders use a spinning metal blade to grind coffee, as you probably guessed by the name. Not much suspense there.

These tend to be cylindrical plastic devices that cost around $15 USD. Don't be lured by the price, though; these grinders have two major drawbacks. First, the coffee is not ground evenly, so you can't get a perfect grind out of them. Second, the blade imparts quite a bit of heat the coffee, which is detrimental to the flavor.

For those reasons, I recommend buying a decent burr grinder if possible. If you can't or don't want to spend much on a grinder, then go with a blade grinder—it will make better coffee than using pre-ground beans.

GRINDER FEATURES TO CONSIDER

SPEED

Most grinders work at a reasonable speed, but if you have your eye on a certain model you should check out some reviews and see if anyone complains about the speed (or lack thereof) before you make a purchase.

DOSER

A doser on a grinder is a large cylinder in the front of the grinder that receives the grounds. Not all grinders have one, and it makes preparing espresso easier because you to lock your portafilter into it and do something else while it fills with grounds.

GRIND SETTING

All burr grinders have some type of grind setting adjustment. Some grinders don't allow much adjustment, however, so you should make sure you get one that fits your needs.

WHAT ELSE SHOULD YOU LOOK FOR IN GRINDERS?

Static, noise, safety, and ease of cleaning are important factors to consider when buying a grinder.

NOISE

Some grinders are extremely loud, which can be very annoying. The Capresso conical burr grinders (Infinity) and the Capresso blade grinders (Cool Grind) are among the least noisy.

SAFETY

Blade grinders cannot operate without the lid in place. In addition, the Capresso Cool Grind series has the fastest blade stopping action of any blade grinder on the market.

Most burr grinders will not grind when there are no beans present, regardless if the grinder is open or closed. The Capresso conical burr grinders will not grind if the bean container is missing or not "locked" in place.

EASE OF CLEANING

Most grinders come with a cleaning brush and have removable upper burrs for easy cleaning of the grinding chamber.

TIME TO GET A GRINDER!

Fit a top-notch grinder into your coffee budget. Trust me, it'll make such a difference in your coffee that you won't regret it! You can get a good conical burr grinder for $100 – $200, and it's well worth it.

If you want to see which brands and models I recommend, I maintain a list of good grinders at www.makingespresso.com.

3

DON'T FORGET THE WATER!

CRAPPY WATER MAKES CRAPPY COFFEE. Metals, chemicals, and minerals can all ruin your espresso regardless of how good your blend, machines, grinder, and skills are.

My choice for water filtration is an under-the-counter reverse osmosis system. Reverse-osmosis produces clean, crisp, and contaminant-free water, and good entry-level systems cost only $200-300. The only recurring expense is changing a filter every 6 months or so ($35).

If you don't want to spend that much, you can get cheap but effective filters from companies like Pur and Brita.

4

THE LITTLE-KNOWN SECRETS OF MAKING GREAT COFFEE

BREWING COFFEE IS A MIXTURE of art and science. It has a long, rich history of diverse methods and equipment, and only a few have gained worldwide popularity. I'm going to explain the methods I use, which I've found to consistently extract the most flavors out of beans while minimizing the extraction of bitter and other undesirable elements.

COFFEE BREWING 101

Brewing consists of dissolving flavors from the coffee grounds in water.

When discussing brewing, the *extraction* is the percentage of grounds that are dissolved in water (the actual solids that mix with the water). *Strength* refers to how concentrated or watery the coffee is. *Brew ratio* is the ratio of coffee grounds (in grams or ounces) to water (in liters or half-gallons).

Professor E.E. Lockhart computed in the 1950s that the ideal extraction percentage is 18–22%—that is, ideal coffee has 18–22% of the grounds dissolved into the water. If under 18% of the grounds are dissolved, the coffee will be sour and unbalanced due to acids being extracted early, followed by sugars. If over 22% of the grounds are dissolved, the coffee will be bitter as bitter elements extract after the acids and sugars.

The extraction process is governed by four factors: water temperature, brew time, grind size, and method. Smaller grinds extract faster than larger grinds. Water that is too cold will fail to extract certain desirable flavors, while water that's too hot will extract undesirable, bitter elements. A French press uses large grinds and thus requires 3–4 minutes to properly extract coffee, whereas filter coffee has smaller grinds and brews faster. Espresso grinds are even smaller and require only 20–30 seconds of brewing time.

WATER TEMPERATURE

The ideal water temperature for brewing coffee is between 195 °F and 205 °F, which is slightly below boiling (212 °F). The easiest way to do this is to bring water to a boil and then let it come off boiling slightly.

BREW RATIO

To achieve optimal results, use two tablespoons of coffee grounds per six ounces of filtered water. Make sure to use filtered water or spring water as tap water will impart undesirable flavors into the coffee. Distilled water shouldn't be used either as it lacks certain minerals that bring out the natural flavors of the coffee.

BREW METHOD

You have several options for brewing great coffee.

French Press:

I believe that this is the best way to perfectly extract coffee and enjoy unparalleled flavor. The French press allows you to precisely control the extraction time and also delivers flavorful oils that get caught in paper filters. Furthermore, it's also the least expensive coffee brewer available.

The only downside to a French press is that it doesn't afford the convenience of a drip brewer in terms of brewing and cleaning time. These issues are negligible, I think, when you compare the quality of the coffee brewed by these methods (the French press makes *way* better coffee).

Bodum is pretty much universally recognized as the best manufacturer of French presses. I recommend you get an insulated model as this minimizes heat loss during the extraction process.

Here's how to properly brew coffee with a French press:

1. Warm the carafe (beaker) by filling it with hot water. Let it sit for a minute or so while your brew water heats.

2. Warm the filter assembly by placing it into the water heating the carafe. This will improve the quality of the coffee because a cold filter assembly will sap heat from the brewing water, which, in turn, lowers extraction temperature.

3. Heat the filtered brewing water in the way noted above.

4. Pour the water from the carafe and put in the ground coffee.

5. Pour in the brewing water and put the plunger in place, but do not press it down yet. Make sure the lid is secure to prevent heat loss.

6. Let it steep for about 4 minutes (2–3 minutes if you're using a fine grind). To ensure complete saturation, some people stir the grounds about 30–60 seconds after adding the water, or they add about a third of the brewing water, wait 20–30 seconds, and then add the rest (this is what I do).

7. When the brewing time is up, push down the plunger to trap the grounds at the bottom, and pour off the coffee (don't drink it from the brewing vessel as it will continue to steep and become bitter and over-extracted).

If the plunger sticks, don't try to force it. Just back it up to the top and try again. If the problem continues, you've either used too fine a grind or your grinder is dumping excessive dust into your grounds (gross). Both of these things choke the filter and make the plunger stick as the water can't pass through it.

Vacuum Coffee Pot:

This clever little device has been around since its invention in the 1830s and it still makes an excellent cup of coffee. It's a great option if you don't like the sediment at the bottom of a cup produced by a French press.

It works by heating water in a lower vessel until expansion forces the contents through a narrow tube into an upper vessel containing coffee grounds. The device is then removed from the heat source, the lower vessel's temperature drops, and liquid (coffee) is sucked back down through the tube, which contains a filter that prevents the grounds from following. (I'm sorry if this sounds confusing—if you hop on YouTube you can see many videos that show this in action.)

Once again, I recommend the Bodum brand of vacuum pots. They make high-quality, reliable products, and they even sell electric vacuum pots, which greatly simplify the process.

Here's how you brew coffee in a vacuum pot:

1. Add the proper amount of filtered water to the bottom bulb.

2. Attach the filter to the upper bulb and fit it tightly over the bottom glass bulb.

3. Place the vacuum coffee pot on the stove, making sure that the outside of the bottom bulb is completely dry.

4. Add the grounds (I recommend a medium grind) when the water begins to fill the upper chamber. Leave the pot on the stove for 3–4 minutes and then place on a hot pad.

Within 30 seconds, the lower pot should cool enough to form a vacuum that pulls the brewing coffee into the lower chamber, separating it from the grounds. Play around with the heating and cooling cycles until the total extraction time is 4–5 minutes.

Automatic Drip Coffee Maker:

While this is the easiest way to brew coffee, it also has significant disadvantages. Most drip machines brew at the wrong temperature for the wrong period of time, making horrible coffee even from the best beans.

If you must use a drip brewer, I recommend one produced by TechniVorm. At the time of this writing, their MoccaMaster Clubline KB 741, with the insulated carafe, is probably the best drip brewer available. I can't lie—it makes good coffee.

I don't think it's necessary to explain the simple steps of how to operate a drip brewer, but here are a few tips to help you get the best possible coffee from one:

Place a thick paper filter in the brewing cone (basket) and thoroughly wet it with water. This helps remove the paper taste from the filter.

Don't leave the carafe on the heating plate after the coffee is brewed as continued heat will make the coffee bitter. Instead, pour the coffee into an insulated carafe to help maintain an optimal serving temperature.

Shake the basket as water pours over the grounds to ensure the water extracts the coffee evenly. It also helps to have a machine with a showerhead design for dispersing the water over the grounds instead of a single spout.

SUMMARY

That's it for brewing great coffee! Pretty simple, right? I'm sure you're excited to start trying out various beans and blends and brewing techniques, and so you should be! I think you'll find a whole new coffee experience and become even more enamored with this wonderful nectar.

Next, I want to share with you a collection of my favorite coffee recipes. We'll cover the classics along with some more exotic drinks and even the holiday treats offered by coffee chains.

So let's get started!

5

10 CLASSIC COFFEE DRINKS THAT ARE TO DIE FOR

THE FIRST DRINKS I WANT TO share with you are staples of my everyday coffee drinking. If you haven't tried any of these yet, I suggest you do, because I think you'll find quite a few are worth coming back to again and again.

"JUST RIGHT" ICED COFFEE

Chances are you've had iced coffee that was too sweet, creamy, or watery. As simple as it may seem, a good iced coffee can actually be tricky to make.

A big part of making good iced coffee is using coffee ice cubes. It takes an extra step of preparation, but doing so will ensure your coffee doesn't become a watered-down coffee wannabe. Another key to making good iced coffee is to brew the coffee and then let it cool in the refrigerator for at least two hours. If you use hot, freshly brewed coffee, it will melt the ice cubes instantly.

Makes one serving

Ingredients

1 cup of chilled coffee (refrigerated for at least 2 hours)

1 cup of ice cubes

5 ounces of sweetened condensed milk

Directions

1. Pour chilled coffee into a large cup.

2. Add coffee ice cubes and sweetened condensed milk. Sweeten to taste.

CAFÉ CRÈME

Fresh coffee and a bit of cream never fails to satisfy. I included this because the proportion of coffee to cream is the key to doing it right.

Makes one serving

Ingredients

4 ounces of freshly brewed coffee

1 tablespoon of cream

Directions

1. Mix and serve.

MOCHA COFFEE

This simple, sweet coffee is loved by coffee drinkers everywhere (who also tend to love chocolate). You can make this drink as chocolaty as you want by adding more or less cocoa powder. You can also use a chocolate-flavored creamer if you want even more of a dessert kind of taste.

Makes one serving

Ingredients

1 cup of freshly brewed coffee

1 tablespoon of cocoa powder

1 tablespoon of sugar (or other sweetener)

2 tablespoons of milk (fat-free optional)

Directions

1. Pour freshly brewed coffee into serving cup.

2. Stir in cocoa powder, sugar (or other sweetener), and milk.

SPICED MOCHA COFFEE

This is a lovely little variation on mocha coffee that involves mixing spices into the coffee grounds before brewing. Doing this gives wonderful notes of flavor without overpowering the cup.

Makes one serving

Ingredients

1/4 cup of coffee grounds

3/4 teaspoon of ground cinnamon

1/4 teaspoon of nutmeg

2 tablespoons of brown sugar (or other sweetener)

2 ounces of chocolate syrup

1/2 teaspoon of vanilla extract

1 3/4 cups of filtered water

Dollop of whipped cream (optional)

Directions

1. Place the grounds, cinnamon, and nutmeg in the coffee maker and brew the coffee as described in the previous chapter.

2. Once the coffee is brewed, remove the carafe from the heat plate and stir in the milk, sugar, vanilla extract, and chocolate syrup. Top with whipped cream (optional) and serve.

CAFÉ AU LAIT

Café au Lait is a simple drink that consists of equal parts of freshly brewed coffee and steamed milk. The key to a delicious au Lait, however, is properly "double brewing" your coffee. What's that? "Double-brewed coffee" is coffee prepared in such a way that it is significantly stronger than normal brewing.

One way of doing this is running already brewed coffee back through the coffee maker with another batch of fresh grounds (using brewed coffee in the water reservoir). I don't recommend this method, however, because it produces strange-tasting coffee. By reheating the coffee, you lose flavor and the end product has a bitter aftertaste.

The double-brewing method I recommend is achieved by simply using twice the normal amount of grounds for the water you're using (with the normal extraction time). That is, four tablespoons of grounds for every six ounces of water. This creates coffee with a strong, bold flavor, which is perfect for the Café au Lait.

Makes one serving

Ingredients

4 ounces of double-brewed coffee

4 ounces of milk, steamed (fat-free optional)

Directions

1. Brew the coffee and remove it from the heating plate.

2. If you don't have a machine to steam milk, heat a small saucepan over medium heat. Pour the milk into it. Heat the milk for 3–4 minutes, stirring constantly to avoid a milk crust.

3. Once the milk steams, take it off the stove and pour, at the same time, both the milk and coffee into a serving cup.

VANILLA COFFEE LATTE

A real latte is made with espresso, but this drink uses double-brewed coffee, which also makes for a yummy beverage.

Makes one serving

Ingredients

4 ounces of fresh double-brewed coffee

2 tablespoons of sugar (or other sweetener)

1/4 teaspoon of vanilla extract

4 ounces of milk (fat-free optional)

Ground cinnamon or grated chocolate, to taste

Directions

1. Stir the sugar and vanilla extract into the coffee.

2. Pour the milk into a medium-sized jar with a lid and shake vigorously for 30 seconds. Remove the lid and microwave the milk for about 30 seconds, or until foam forms on the top.

3. Pour the milk into the coffee and spoon the foam onto the top of the beverage. Top with ground cinnamon or grated chocolate.

FRAPPUCCINO

If you love a Starbucks Frappuccino but don't love the price, why not make your own? This recipe will taste just like the real deal for a fraction of the cost.

Makes one serving

Ingredients

6 ounces of chilled, double-brewed coffee (refrigerated for at least 2 hours)

1 cup of milk (fat-free optional)

3 tablespoons of sugar (or other sweetener)

2 cups of ice cubes

Caramel sauce, to taste (optional)

Chocolate sauce, to taste (optional)

Whipped cream, to taste (optional)

Directions

1. Put everything in a blender and blend on high until a slushy consistency.

FROSTY DELIGHT

This is a smooth, refreshing drink that's great for a hot summer day.

Makes one serving

Ingredients

4 ounces of chilled, double-brewed coffee (refrigerated for at least 2 hours)

2 ounces of milk (fat-free optional)

1 tablespoon of sweetened condensed milk

3/4 cup of ice cubes

2–3 tablespoons of sugar (or other sweetener)

Directions

1. Put everything in a blender and blend on high until a slushy consistency.

SPICED ORANGE COFFEE

This is a wonderfully flavorful drink that can be served hot and cold (poured over ice).

Makes one serving

Ingredients

2 tablespoons of coffee grounds

1 teaspoon of grated orange peel

1/2 teaspoon of cinnamon

1/4 teaspoon of nutmeg

5 whole cloves

1 tablespoon of brown sugar (or other sweetener)

1 cup of filtered water

Whipped cream (optional)

Directions

1. Combine the coffee grounds, grated orange zest, cloves, and cinnamon in a small bowl and then use to brew your coffee.

2. Once the coffee is brewed, stir and top with whipped cream if desired.

VIENNESE COFFEE

This is one of my favorite "dessert-in-a-cup" indulgences. Truly a drink to savor.

Ingredients

1 cup of freshly brewed coffee

1 tablespoon of heavy whipping cream

1 ounce of semisweet chocolate, finely chopped

Pinch of cinnamon

Whipped cream

Directions

1. Brew the coffee.

2. Heat the cream and chocolate in a small saucepan over low heat, stirring constantly. Once the chocolate has melted, remove from heat, pour in the coffee and stir well. Pour into a mug and garnish with whipped cream and cinnamon.

6

7 HOLIDAY COFFEE DRINKS THAT WILL MAKE YOU CHEER

THE HOLIDAYS CAN BE STRESSFUL and overwhelming, but they're also a great time to be a coffee drinker! In this chapter I'm going to share my favorite holiday treats. Enjoy!

PUMPKIN SPICED COFFEE LATTE

It's hard not to fall in love with this Starbucks creation. I make my own so I don't go completely broke every winter. Don't be surprised if you become famous in your family for these wonderful beverages.

Makes one serving
Ingredients

2 tablespoons of coffee grounds

1 cup of milk (fat-free optional)

1 teaspoon of sugar (or other sweetener)

Dash of vanilla extract

1/2 teaspoon of pumpkin spice

1/2 teaspoon of allspice

1/4 teaspoon of cinnamon

1 cup of filtered water

Cream, to taste (optional)

Directions

1. Combine the coffee grounds, pumpkin spice, allspice, and cinnamon in a small bowl and then use to brew your coffee.

2. Once the coffee is brewed, add the vanilla extract and mix in cream and sugar, if desired.

HOMEMADE NOGGED COFFEE

You know the holidays have arrived when eggnog finds its way into peoples' fridges. This classic Christmas drink is a perfect way to get your fix.

Ingredients

4 ounces of fresh double-brewed coffee

2/3 cup of eggnog

1/3 cup of milk, steamed (fat-free optional)

Sugar (or other sweetener), to taste

Whipped cream (optional)

Nutmeg (optional)

1 shot of rum (optional)

Directions

1. If you don't have a machine to steam milk, heat a small saucepan over medium heat. Pour the eggnog and milk into it. Heat the mixture for 3–4 minutes, stirring constantly.

2. Once the mixture steams, combine it in a mug with the coffee.

3. Top with whipped cream and nutmeg, if desired.

TRADITIONAL IRISH COFFEE

This winter drink is a great for entertaining guests or when you want to add a bit of kick to your coffee experience. To help ensure the whipped cream floats, use a warm spoon to place it and do so lightly so it doesn't break the surface of the coffee.

Ingredients

6 ounces of freshly brewed coffee

1 teaspoon of brown sugar (or other sweetener)

1 1/2 ounces of your favorite Irish whiskey (I like Redbreast)

Dollop of whipped cream

Directions

1. Immediately after your coffee is brewed, mix in the whiskey and brown sugar. Mix well until the sugar dissolves.

2. Put the dollop of whipped cream on the top of the beverage.

GINGERBREAD COFFEE LATTE

When the fireplaces come to life and you can see your breath in the morning, keep warm with this spicy latte.

Ingredients

2 ounces of freshly brewed espresso

2 tablespoons of gingerbread-flavored syrup

1/2 cup of milk, steamed (fat-free optional)

Dollop of whipped cream

Pinch of ground nutmeg

Pinch of ground cinnamon

1/2 teaspoon of vanilla powder

Directions

1. If you don't have a machine to steam milk, heat a small saucepan over medium heat. Pour the milk into it. Heat the milk for 3–4 minutes, stirring constantly to avoid a milk crust.

2. Once the milk steams, take it off the stove and pour both the milk and coffee at the same time into a serving cup.

3. Combine the espresso and flavored syrup in a coffee mug. Stir well.

4. Pour the steamed milk into the coffee mixture and top with whipped cream. Sprinkle nutmeg, cinnamon, and vanilla powder on top.

PEPPERMINT MOCHA

This is one of Starbucks' winter exclusives and it's really good. Who wants to wait all year and pay $5 a pop, though? Here's how to make your own.

Ingredients

3 tablespoons of powdered baking cocoa

3 tablespoons of warm water

1 1/2 tablespoons of peppermint syrup (don't use peppermint extract—get syrup from Starbucks) OR 1 1/2 tablespoons of crème de menthe

4 ounces of freshly brewed espresso

1 cup of milk, steamed (fat-free optional)

Dollop of whipped cream

Directions

1. Combine the baking cocoa with the warm water. Stir until it has a syrupy consistency. Pour into a coffee mug.

2. Pour in the espresso and mix well.

3. Pour in the peppermint syrup or crème de menthe and mix well.

4. Pour in the steamed milk and mix well.

5. Place dollop of whipped cream on top.

SPICY CHOCOLATE MOCHA

This is a chocolate mocha drink with a spicy twist. If you like a little heat in your food, I think you'll really like this recipe.

Ingredients

4 ounces of freshly brewed espresso

4 ounces of milk (fat-free optional)

1 small, dried red chili (such as chile de àrbol)

1/2 of a cinnamon stick

Couple pinches of sugar (or other sweetener)

Couple pinches of unsweetened cocoa powder

Dollop of whipped cream

Directions

1. Combine the milk, chili, and cinnamon stick in a large saucepan. Bring to a simmer over high heat.

2. Once simmering, remove from heat and cover for 15 minutes.

3. Brew your espresso once the milk mixture has sat for about 10 minutes.

4. Combine the espresso, sugar, and cocoa powder with the milk mixture. Mix well.

5. Bring the mixture to a simmer over high heat, stirring constantly. Once simmering, remove from heat. Discard the cinnamon sticks and chili.

6. Pour into a mug and place the dollop of whipped cream on top.

POLAR ESPRESSO

This is a delicious holiday drink with a bit of zing. Give it a try!

Ingredients

2 ounces of espresso, chilled for at least 2 hours

1 1/2 ounces of white-chocolate liqueur

1/2 ounce of peppermint schnapps

1 1/2 ounces of half-and-half

Cocoa powder

Whipped cream

Directions

1. Fill a cocktail shaker with ice and add the espresso, liqueur, schnapps, and half-and-half. Shake until fully mixed.

2. Top with whipped cream and cocoa powder.

7

5 COFFEE DESSERT DRINKS THAT ARE LIKE HEAVEN IN A CUP

OKAY, SO MAYBE COFFEE PURISTS wouldn't call these "proper" coffee drinks, but sometimes we need to satisfy our sweet tooth, and coffee can sure make some great "desserts in a cup."

Do yourself a favor and splurge on one of these every now and then!

<u>CAFÉ LIÉGEOIS</u>

This is one of my favorite coffee dessert indulgences. Absolutely delicious.

<u>Ingredients</u>

1 scoop of vanilla or coffee ice cream

4 ounces of double-brewed coffee, chilled for at least 2 hours

Dollop of whipped cream

<u>Directions</u>

1. Put the ice cream in a glass and pour the coffee over it. Top with whipped cream.

VANILLA BANANA COFFEE MILKSHAKE

This may sound quite strange, but it's actually quite good. The combination of banana, vanilla, and coffee is very tasty.

Ingredients

1/2 banana

2 tablespoons of sugar

1 cup of double-brewed coffee, chilled for at least 2 hours

1/2 cup of vanilla ice cream

Directions

1. Put the banana in a blender and blend on high until a smooth "paste."

2. Put the rest of the ingredients in the blender and blend on high until the mixture has the consistency of a milkshake.

FRULATTE

If you like fruit shakes, you'll love this fruit milkshake with a hint of coffee. (Try it as a post-workout drink!)

Ingredients

4 ounces of coffee, chilled for at least 2 hours

1 1/2 cups of ice cubes

4 ounces of milk (fat-free optional)

1/2 cup of peach or strawberry chunks

1/4 teaspoon of vanilla extract

Directions

1. Put all the ingredients in a blender and blend on high until the mixture has the consistency of a milkshake.

JAMAICAN COFFEE

This is a tropical variation of Irish coffee and it makes a great after-dinner treat.

Ingredients

1 ounce of dark rum

1 ounce of coffee-flavored liqueur

1 cup of freshly brewed coffee

Dollop of whipped cream

Directions

1. Pour the rum and liqueur into a glass. Mix in the coffee and garnish with whipped cream.

MOCHA FRAPPÉ

People rave about these types of frozen coffee drinks and I understand why! I am obsessed with Mocha coffee, so I had to include this.

Ingredients

4 ounces of freshly brewed coffee

4 ounces of milk

1 tablespoon of chocolate syrup

1 tablespoon of sugar (or other sweetener)

Directions

1. Pour the coffee into an ice cube tray and freeze until solid.

2. Once the coffee is frozen, combine it with the rest of the ingredients in a blender. Blend on high until the mixture has a slushy consistency.

8

WELCOME TO THE TANTALIZING WORLD OF ESPRESSO

WHAT IS ESPRESSO? THE NAME *espresso* is Italian in origin. It was first coined around 1900 and, loosely translated, means a cup of coffee brewed expressly (just) for you. Today, you will often find that people incorrectly pronounce or spell it "expresso." Many think that cappuccino and latte are the same as espresso (they aren't).

What makes a true espresso?

Is it the bean?

No. Marketing and word of mouth has led people to believe that the type of bean determines whether a brew is espresso or not. This isn't true. Any type of bean can be used to make good espresso.

Is it the blend?

No. Although there are blends of beans created just for espresso, the blend doesn't make it espresso. The pursuit of the perfect espresso blend has led to this common misunderstanding. Some roasters say that you can only make a good espresso with the right blend.

Is it the roast?

No. Some think that espresso must be an extremely dark roast; however, the espresso roast varies from region to region. In California, you will see a dark or "French" roast. On the East Coast, a light roast is common. And in northern Italy, a medium roast is normally used. Any roast can be used to make good espresso. It is simply a matter of taste.

Are all espresso machines really espresso machines?

No. There are machines out there sold as "espresso machines" that aren't true espresso machines. These machines are usually electric "moka" style machines that use steam pressure to force water through the ground beans. Steam pressure can only produce up to about 1.5 bar or 50 psi (pounds per square inch) of pressure. A real espresso machine must produce at least 9 bar or 135 psi to force the water through the finely ground and compacted ground beans. Steam-driven moka machines are often sold in major department stores for $75 or less.

So, what is espresso?

Espresso coffee is a small (1–2 oz.) shot of pressure-brewed coffee, using about 7 grams (or one tablespoon) of finely ground coffee.

When done properly, extraction takes about 20 – 25 seconds and the coffee will feature a layer of rich, dark golden cream, called crema on the surface. This crema is one indicator of a quality espresso.

Making good espresso coffee is an art and science unto itself and quite different from what you just learned about brewing great coffee.

I actually wrote a book just on making espresso called *How to Make Espresso So Good You'll Never Waste Money on Starbucks Again*. If you're not sure how to make rich, rewarding espresso, then I recommend you pick it up for a few bucks and learn! It's an easy, quick read, and you'll learn a lot!

9

HOW TO SPEAK LIKE AN ESPRESSO LOVER

LIKE ANY OTHER FIELD OF knowledge, espresso has its own little language that you should know. Below is a small list of key words that you'll often hear and will need to know in order to understand how to make killer espresso.

Bar: Pressure rating used on most pump driven espresso machines. 9 bars, the typical accepted pressure for brewing espresso is 8.8 atmospheres of pressure or 130 pounds per square inch. Almost every consumer espresso machine is capable of producing this pressure consistently.

Brew Group: The area of the machine that contains the *grouphead* and *portafilter* and *filter baskets* (see these words in this glossary). Some brew groups are actively heated by an electrical heating mechanism, and some are passively heated by the water boiler through metal-on-metal contact. The entire brew group needs to be sufficiently heated in order to brew a proper espresso.

Burr Grinder: The recommended type of grinder for proper espresso making. A burr grinder features two disks, one stationary, one rotating, which slice away portions of a coffee bean into very fine particles. It's called a "burr" grinder because a "burr" is a rough edge that protrudes from something.

Crema: The dark, golden-brown layer resembling foam on top of an espresso shot. This liquid contains oils and is one of the sure signs of a properly brewed shot of espresso. It's created by the high-pressure dispersion of gases (air and carbon dioxide) in the coffee.

Demitasse: The cup that holds a traditional shot of espresso is called a demitasse. It's a fancy word for a 3-ounce (or smaller) cup. Demitasses can be made of ceramic, stainless steel, or glass, though porcelain is often the preferred material. The thicker the better, as they retain the beverage's heat well.

Dispersion Screen: A part of an espresso machine that serves the purpose of properly dispersing (spreading) brewing water over the portafilter and filter basket (you will learn what these are in a minute), ensuring the entire coffee bed is saturated with water uniformly.

Dosage: The amount of ground coffee used to produce a shot of espresso. A single dosage is 7 grams of coffee grounds, which makes 1.5 ounces of espresso (which is a single shot of espresso).

Doser: This is found on many burr grinders, and it releases a measure of coffee grounds as you pull on a lever. It gives you a proper dosage of coffee grounds.

Filter Basket: A metal, flat bottomed "bowl" shaped insert that fits inside a portafilter. The filter basket holds your ground coffee and has a lot of tiny holes in the bottom to allow the extracted beverage to seep through and pour into a demitasse cup or other receptacle.

Most espresso machines include two filter baskets—a single basket and a double basket (for making single and double shots)—though some machines feature convertible baskets that allow either a single or double shot of espresso to be produced from the same basket.

Frothing Tip: The perforated tip on a steaming wand. These can have between one and four holes, and the holes can be either angled to the side or pointing straight down. They allow the steam from the espresso machine to be forced into tiny jets, which heat and froth milk.

Group Head: The part of an espresso machine that contains the locking connector for the portafilter and the dispersion screen. These are usually made out of brass, but sometimes other materials such as stainless steel or aluminum are used. The grouphead maintains temperature stability in the machine, which is essential for producing a perfect shot of espresso.

Portafilter: (Also known as a *groupo*.) The device that holds a filter basket and attaches to an espresso machine. High-quality portafilters are made of copper or brass, and are coated with chrome. The handles are usually covered in wood, ceramic, or plastic.

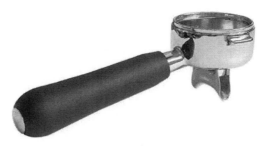

Pull: A term used to describe brewing a shot of espresso. The term comes from the fact that machines of the 50s and 60s included a lever that you had to pull to engage the machine.

Steam Wand: A visible, external pipe found on most espresso machines that is used to froth and steam milk, to provide hot water (on some machines), and heat espresso cups. Some also use the steam wand to heat water. It is controlled by a steam knob that opens and closes the steam valve inside the machine.

Shot: Another term to describe 1.5 ounces of brewed espresso.

Tamping: The act of pressing and compacting a bed of loose, finely ground coffee into the portafilter in preparation for brewing espresso. The purpose of tamping grounds is to create a coffee "puck" (as it's called) in the filter basket that is even in depth and density and that has no gaps or breaks around the perimeter. This ensures even distribution of the water, which is necessary for high-quality espresso.

The classic "tamp" is to press straight down onto the coffee grounds with about 30 pounds of pressure, followed by a light twist to fully settle the grounds. Another common "tamp" is about 10 pounds of pressure on very finely ground beans.

Tamper: The device used to tamp a bed of loose coffee grounds in a portafilter in preparation for brewing espresso. Most espresso machines include a plastic tamper as an accessory, but metal tampers can be bought. They are measured in millimeters, corresponding with the diameter of the filter basket. Most commercial and high-end consumer espresso machines use a 58mm tamper; other common sizes are 49mm, 53mm, and 57mm.

Thermoblock: In some espresso machines, the heating system is shaped similar to that of a car radiator: A series of heated metal coils or channels which water must pass through and become progressively hotter as it reaches the boiler.

10

THE 8 KEYS TO MAKING KILLER ESPRESSO

FANTASTIC ESPRESSO IS SWEET, IT has a potent aroma, and a rich, strong flavor. The crema should be dark reddish-brown and smooth, yet thick. A perfect espresso should be enjoyable straight with no additives and bold enough to not disappear in milk. A pleasant and aromatic aftertaste should linger for several minutes after drinking it.

Let's take a look at the art and science of espresso making from a birds-eye view. We'll first look at each of the major factors briefly and then get into the details each.

The major factors in making great espresso are (in no particular order)…

THE BEANS

A great espresso starts with great beans. This means fresh beans that are properly roasted and blended for the right amount of sweetness, aromatics, and smoothness.

THE MACHINE

Your machine plays a huge role in the quality of your espresso. It is definitely not true that "an espresso machine is an espresso machine." All other things being the same, some machines make great coffee while others don't.

Price, however, isn't a safe way to choose a machine. Some $500 machines make better espresso than $1,000 machines. Choosing the right machine is one of the most important steps and in this book, I'll help you find the perfect machine for your needs.

If you don't want to buy an expensive machine, that's okay too! You can use inexpensive manual devices like stovetop makers and "piston-style" machines, which we will go over too. I have to be honest though: These inexpensive machines can't match the quality of higher-end models.

THE GRINDER

To make great espresso, you must be able to grind the coffee very finely because you'll be packing it very tightly into the filter basket. If the grinds aren't very fine, they won't pack tight and the water will flow too easily through them (resulting in watered-down, horrible espresso).

A standard coffee grinder will not do. A high quality burr grinder is essential for espresso. A conical burr grinder is preferred over flat burrs (conical burrs curve upwards while flat burrs don't) since the particle size is more even, they last longer, and the coffee is not heated during the grinding process (which diminishes the aroma of the coffee). A conical/flat hybrid blade is considered the best design by many coffee professionals.

THE WATER

The water used for espresso must be filtered (as should all water we drink, really). Don't use unfiltered tap water because it will pass on undesirable tastes to the coffee, and don't use distilled water because it lacks the minerals of naturally-derived water that add to the taste of the coffee.

You should dump your tanks daily and start with fresh water if you want optimal tasting espresso.

THE PREPARATION AND EXTRACTION

Ideal extraction time for one shot of espresso is between 25 – 30 seconds. There are several things you must do correctly to achieve this, and we'll be covering them soon.

THE ESPRESSO CUP

The espresso cup should be pre-heated from a source other than the espresso machine. Filling a cup with water from the espresso machine prior to brewing the espresso will lower the temperature of the water in the boiler and the espresso extraction will be uneven. The espresso cup should have thick walls and a narrow mouth to retain heat and aroma.

ESPRESSO MACHINE AND GRINDER CLEANLINESS

Coffee machine cleaning is probably the biggest problem with espresso today. If the machine, basket, and portafilter are not cleaned regularly, the espresso will taste rancid.

Every day the burr blades should be swept clean. Between shots you may want to brush out the excess espresso that gets stuck between the burrs and the dosing chamber. The burrs must be replaced at least yearly so that they continue to produce good coffee grounds.

PRACTICE!

Everyone knows that practice makes perfect, and that applies to making espresso. If you just do it regularly, you might be surprised at how you continue to make better and better espresso. Many times I made a shot that I thought was so good I couldn't possibly do better, and several cups later, I was amazed again.

11

HOW TO PULL THE PERFECT SHOT OF ESPRESSO

WE'VE FINALLY REACHED THE *SEXY* part of making espresso: preparing and pulling the shot.

Extracting espresso is part art and part science. The art is understanding the nuances of your coffee, grinder and espresso machine. The science is applying specific techniques to the coffee roast, fineness of grind, tamp pressure, temperature, brew pressure and extraction time.

The best way to learn how to make espresso is to begin with the techniques. As you continue to make espresso, you'll gradually learn the "art."

THE GOLDEN RULE OF MAKING ESPRESSO

The golden rule of making espresso is very simple: a single shot of espresso equals 1 – 1.5 fluid ounces of coffee that was pulled through approximately 7 – 10 grams of tamped coffee grounds in about 20 – 25 seconds. Purists say that you should use 7 grams of grounds for every ounce of espresso. There are 8 fluid ounces in a cup and 7 grams of ground coffee is about 1 tablespoon of grounds.

The extraction time is very important— if it takes more or less than 20-25 seconds to brew one shot, the flavor of the beverage will suffer. Incorrect grinding or tamping causes this—something we'll get more into soon.

As a note, a double shot equals 2 – 2.5 fluid ounces of coffee that was pulled through approximately 14 grams of ground coffee in about 20-25 seconds.

Alright, let's take a deeper look at the different things that affect the quality of your coffee extraction.

ESPRESSO BREWING BASICS

BREWING TEMPERATURE

This is controlled by your machine's thermostat. All good machines heat water to the proper temperature range, which is approximately 190 – 196 degrees.

The "in-cup" temperature of coffee should be around 160 – 165 degrees. This temperature will feel hot to the lips but not scalding.

To ensure that you get the proper "in-cup" temperature, you should preheat the cup. The cup can be heated several ways: a cup warmer on the espresso machine, hot water from the espresso machine, or even hot water from your faucet.

You should also heat the brew group (the portafilter and group head). To do this, I suggest that you run a few ounces of hot water through the group with the portafilter in place (without coffee) and into the cup. It is the most efficient method and the second shot is always better than the first anyway!

BREW PRESSURE

This is the amount of pressure developed when extracting the coffee. We look at approximately 8 to 9 bars as being the optimum environment. You may have noticed that some home machines show pressure ratings of 15 to 19 bars. This is an indication of the maximum pressure the pump is capable of producing, but machines are designed these days to not allow any more than 8 to 11 bars.

Remember that the machine alone does not ensure the right pressure when brewing coffee—it only ensures that you do not use too much pressure. Even if your machine can produce the 8-9 bars necessary, you can still end up with weak, under-extracted coffee. How? By having insufficient resistance in the brew group. You create resistance by properly grinding and tamping your coffee. A finer grind of coffee and strong tamp pressure leads to more resistance, which helps you get that golden espresso.

TAMP PRESSURE

This is the amount of force that you apply to compact the coffee grounds that you have placed in the filter basket. You use a "tamper" that is supplied with most machines.

The basic technique for tamping is to first gently knock the porta-filter with the tamper and then apply about 30 pounds of level pressure, finishing with a twist to polish the top of the exposed coffee grounds.

You can use a bathroom scale and press down with the tamper to get a good sense of what 30 pounds of pressure feels like. Another tip is to lean into the tamp, using your body weight, instead of trying to muscle it with your arm. This will give you a more consistent tamp.

Now, some machines require only a light tamp. Those machines are designed with "pressurized filter handles," which are designed to create resistance despite the light tamp. These systems work very well, but still require that you understand the principles of tamping pressure. Saeco, Capresso and Solis all make machines with this technology.

Machines made by Gaggia, Rancilio, La Pavoni (piston style), and Francis require the user to create the resistance without such aids. They are designed for the user to have control of the tamping, which can help you fine-tune the taste of your coffee

GRINDING

My universal measurement for grind fineness is slightly finer than granulated sugar. When no one is looking, go ahead and stick your fingers in the sugar bowl and get a feel for the grain size.

Incorrectly ground beans can gum up and prematurely wear out the grinder burrs, clog the dispersion screen, and make a bitter cup of coffee out of a great bean.

As your beans get older you will notice that the extraction time will shorten up when everything else remains the same. This is because the bean is drying out, which causes less resistance when tamped and, unfortunately, this is a direct sign that the flavor is drying up as well.

When you are calibrating a grinder, you will usually find that the best espresso grind setting will be in a range of 3 to 8 on the grinder's index. The lower the number, the finer the grind. But do remember, a setting on one grinder will not necessarily match the setting on other grinders in terms of actual results.

In order to reproduce excellent coffee time after time, the grind fineness must be the same. Variation will cause wildly fluctuating extraction times and the coffee quality will suffer.

You know you've nailed it when your coffee grounds conform to the Golden Rule—if you get those results, you're getting the best from the bean.

SPECIAL NOTE

When adjusting your grinder, make sure the grinder is running. This is because the grinding burrs need to move closer for a finer grind. Since coffee is actually a very hard material, if you adjust it with it off, you can stress the adjustment mechanism and actually damage the machine!

STEP-BY-STEP ESPRESSO EXTRACTION

PREHEATING

As you know, it's important that the cup and brew group are preheated before extracting coffee, or they will suck heat from the beverage and interfere with its flavor.

In case you forgot, I recommend that you run a few ounces of hot water through the group with the portafilter in place (without coffee) and into the cup.

EXTRACTION OF A SINGLE SHOT

1. Start with a clean machine, portafiler, and cup.

2. Begin grinding beans by turning on grinder.

3. After you have ground your coffee, place one tablespoon of grounds into the portafilter basket and tamp as we discussed.

    Take a look at the tamped coffee—it should be compacted and the surface level. An uneven surface can cause problems with the extraction so ensure the surface looks polished and any loose coffee grounds around the top of the rim are brushed off. This is prevents the rubber, water-tight seal from getting encrusted with coffee, which can lead to leaking around the brew group and bitter cup of coffee!

4. Pre-heat the cup the beverage will be served in.

5. Attach the portafilter to the machine and place your preheated cup under the beak or dispensing nozzles.

6. With your eye on your watch, press the pump button and watch your extraction carefully. You will see that the first part of the brew

is dark and, if done properly, followed by a golden-brown, foamy mixture that streams gently into your cup. You may even see what we call "mouse tails," which are thin and curly streams of espresso that look like they're barely holding together.

When you have dispensed between 1 and 1.5 ounces, stop the pump and check your time—20 – 25 seconds should have passed. This is the most critical information you need to make adjustments. If you are running long, then you can lighten up on the tamp or go with a coarser grind. My recommendation is to stay with the same tamp (for consistency purposes) and vary the grind fineness.

You will find that there is a world of difference between a 15-second shot and a 20 – 25 second shot. The same can be said for an over-30 second shot. When the extraction time is between 20 – 25 seconds, the crema will be at its thickest consistency, and the coffee's flavor is at its best.

Play around with grinds and tamp pressure to see what makes the best coffee for you, always obeying the Golden Rule. If you tamp lighter with a very fine grind, you can still keep the extraction time to 20 – 25 seconds, and the same goes for a heavier-than-usual tamp with a coarser grind.

TIPS

- Think of your testing as a scientific experiment! Don't vary more than one variable at a time. If you are going to change your grind setting, keep the tamp pressure and coffee dosage consistent.

- Generally speaking, fill the portafilter basket with coffee grounds so that it is loosely full, about to the rim.

- If you are not sure what 30lbs of tamping pressure feels like, get out the bathroom scale. Place a paper towel over the scale and place the portafilter handle with basket in it on the scale and press down with your tamper until the scale reads 30lbs.

IF YOU HAVE A GRINDER:

- If you get 1 – 1.5 ounces of coffee in 10 – 15 seconds, your shot is too fast. Try a finer grind or heavier tamp, testing them one at a time until you achieve the desired results.

- If it takes 30+ seconds to get 1 – 1.5 ounces of coffee, your shot is too slow. Try a coarser grind or lighter tamp.

IF YOU DON'T HAVE A GRINDER:

- If you do not have your own grinder, then you need to tamp harder if your shot is too quick and tamp lighter if it's too slow.

THE DOUBLE SHOT

A double shot of espresso is made by doing everything you've already learned, but using 14 grams (2 tablespoons) of coffee grounds instead of 7 grams. It's very important that the extraction time remain the same—20 – 25 seconds.

Once again, play with tamp pressure and grind settings to achieve this ideal extraction time.

SUMMARY

And that's the whole story of how to make amazing espresso. Why don't you put the book down for a minute and give it a try!

12

8 ESPRESSO DRINKS THAT EVERY COFFEE LOVER SHOULD TRY

WHEN PROPERLY MADE, ESPRESSO IS a heavenly shot of sweet, aromatic coffee bliss topped by a golden crown of beautiful crema. While a perfectly-brewed espresso is *bellisimo* by itself, it also makes some sublime drinks.

The following recipes are my favorites that I find myself making again and again. I hope you enjoy them too!

CLASSIC CAPPUCCINO

The traditional cappuccino is simple: it's three equal parts of espresso, steamed milk, and milk foam. Here's an easy way to make it.

Ingredients

2 ounces of freshly brewed espresso

4 ounces of milk, steamed (fat-free optional)

Directions

1. Brew the espresso.

2. Steam the milk using your machine until about half of it has foamed. If your machine doesn't have a milk steamer, you can microwave the milk in a bowl for about 30 seconds and then whisk it

vigorously until about half of it has foamed.

3. Pour the hot milk under the foam into a mug and then add the espresso. Spoon the foam on top.

CAFÉ CONQUISTADOR

This spiked drink is great for after dinner or parties.

Ingredients

2 ounces of freshly brewed espresso

4 ounces of milk, steamed (fat-free optional)

1 1/2 ounces of coffee liqueur (Kahlua is good)

Directions

1. Brew the espresso.

2. Steam the milk using your machine until about half of it has foamed. If your machine doesn't have a milk steamer, you can microwave the milk in a bowl for about 30 seconds and then whisk it vigorously until about half of it has foamed.

3. Pour the hot milk under the foam into a mug and then add the espresso and liqueur. Spoon the foam on top.

MOCHACCINO

This is a great morning drink that pairs nicely with a breakfast pastry or bagel.

Ingredients

2 ounces of freshly brewed espresso

1 1/2 tablespoons of chocolate syrup

4 ounces of milk, steamed (fat-free optional)

Pinch of cocoa powder

Pinch of cinnamon

Directions

1. Brew the espresso.

2. Steam the milk using your machine until about half of it has foamed. If your machine doesn't have a milk steamer, you can microwave the milk in a bowl for about 30 seconds and then whisk it vigorously until about half of it has foamed.

3. Pour the hot milk under the foam into a mug and then add the espresso and chocolate syrup. Spoon the foam on top. Garnish with cocoa powder and cinnamon.

ICED LATTE

This is a great daily pick-me-up and unlike a coffee latte, you don't need to use coffee ice cubes.

Ingredients

2–4 ounces of freshly brewed espresso (depending on how strong you like it)

8 ounces of milk (fat-free optional)

2 cups of ice cubes

Pinch of sugar (or other sweetener), to taste

Directions

1. Brew the espresso.

2. Put the ice cubes in a container with a lid and pour the espresso over.

3. Add the milk on top, add a lid and shake until thoroughly mixed.

4. Pour into a mug and sweeten with sugar to taste.

Note:

If you want a *frappé*, put everything in a blender and blend on high until a smooth consistency.

CARAMEL MACCHIATO

This Starbucks creation is famous for a good reason: it's tastes absolutely fantastic. Save your money and make it yourself!

Ingredients

2 ounces of freshly brewed espresso

6 ounces of milk, steamed (fat-free optional)

1 teaspoon of vanilla syrup

1 teaspoon of caramel syrup

Dollop of whipped cream (optional)

Directions

1. Steam the milk using your machine until about half of it has foamed. If your machine doesn't have a milk steamer, you can microwave the milk in a bowl for about 30 seconds and then whisk it vigorously until about half of it has foamed.

2. Pour the hot milk from the bottom into a mug. Pour the vanilla and caramel syrups in and mix well. Spoon the foam on top.

3. Pour the espresso into the mixture and drizzle with caramel syrup.

WHITE CHOCOLATE CAFFÈ MOCHA

If you like white chocolate, you'll like this twist on the traditional mocha latte.

Ingredients

2 ounces of freshly brewed espresso

4 ounces of milk, steamed (fat-free optional)

1 1/2 ounces of white chocolate, finely chopped

Directions

1. In a small saucepan, heat the milk and white chocolate over high heat until it simmers. Stir constantly. Once it simmers, reduce the heat and continue to stir until the chocolate has completely melted.

2. Brew the espresso.

3. Steam the milk mixture using your machine until it froths. If your machine doesn't have a milk steamer, you can whisk it vigorously until it froths.

4. Pour the milk mixture into a mug and add the espresso.

CAFFÈ AMERICANO

If you want a full cup of coffee but prefer the taste of espresso, try out the Americano. It has a similar strength as regular coffee, but a different taste.

Ingredients

2 ounces of freshly brewed espresso

8 ounces of hot water

Cream and sugar (or other sweetener), to taste

Directions

1. Brew the espresso and pour into a mug.

2. Add the hot water.

3. Sweeten with cream and sugar as you would a regular cup of coffee.

BLACK EYE

This intense drink will get your heart pumping. If you don't do well with caffeine rushes, don't go here!

Ingredients

4 ounces of freshly brewed espresso

6–8 ounces of freshly brewed coffee

Cream and sugar (or other sweetener), to taste

Directions

1. Pour the coffee into a mug and add cream and sugar to taste.

2. Pour the espresso into the mug.

13

WHAT TO KNOW BEFORE BUYING AN ESPRESSO MACHINE

GREAT BEANS AND GOOD SKILLS will be wasted if your espresso machine is poor.

What makes a good machine though? Should you get a semi-automatic or a super-automatic? What about pod machines, manuals, and stovetops?

By the end of this chapter, you will know espresso machines inside and out and you'll be able to choose the machine *perfect* for you and your needs.

So, let's begin.

SUPER-AUTOMATIC MACHINES

With just the push of a button, super-automatic espresso machines do everything necessary to brew a shot of espresso. They grind whole beans and deposit grounds into the filter, they tamp them and then brew them. Super-automatics have very powerful conical burr grinders with gear reduction systems and lots of settings to control the strength of your brew.

Steaming and frothing milk is very easy with the frothing adaptor that attaches to the steam wands.

These machines are the easiest to use, but they are also the most expensive. Some people say that super-automatic means less control and lower quality brews, but I disagree. In actual testing, I've found these machines produce a very consistent and quality espresso. You do lose some control over the brew pressure and tamping pressure, but this can be compensated for with other features that allow you to adjust the grind settings, doser settings, and serving size.

If you're wondering which super-automatic machines are best, head over to my website at www.makingespresso.com and check out my recommended models.

SEMI-AUTOMATIC MACHINES

Semi-automatic machines are very popular for home use because they are reasonably priced, they produce excellent coffee, and they're fairly easy to use. The main difference between a super- and semi-automatic machine is that the semi-automatic machine doesn't grind the beans. Some super-automatics also rinse and clean themselves, whereas you must rinse and clean a semi-automatic.

Most semi-automatic machines use a boiler to heat water as it passes from a separate water tank, however, some models use a thermoblock system, which heats water instantly and reduces wait time.

Some have an "On/Off" switch that you must push once to start extraction and then push again to stop it. Other semi-automatics only require one push of the button to begin the extraction and then they will automatically stop after a pre-programmed time has passed.

Frothing with semi-automatics is simple with some machines but can require some skill with others. This really depends on whether the machine comes with a frothing adaptor or not. The adaptor makes frothing your milk easy while frothing with a traditional steam wand takes a little bit of practice to perfect.

If you're wondering which semi-automatic machines are best, head over to my website at www.makingespresso.com and check out my recommended models.

MANUAL MACHINES

These old-world style machines look great and reflect the original prototypes invented to create a consistent and flavorful cup of espresso. Also called "piston-style" machines, they were the first models to use a hand pump capable of generating the 8 to 9 atmospheres of pressure that is necessary to force the water through the condensed grounds and make a proper espresso.

These machines are recommended for true coffee aficionados and those who enjoy the process and effort involved in making a cup of espresso the traditional way. These machines are tough to use and require a higher skill level than the automatic machines. They also have a small water tank, making them impractical for large gatherings.

The cleaning and maintenance of manuals is fairly straightforward, but the outer finishes, typically brass, chrome or copper, will require special cleaning solvents to remove tarnishing and fingerprints. The steam wands and frothing adaptors are standard and powerful enough for home use.

It's also worth noting that pulling down the handle to force water through the espresso grounds does require a bit of arm strength and the consistency of the pull is critical to making a quality cup of coffee.

If you're wondering which manual machines are best, head over to my website at www.makingespresso.com and check out my recommended models.

POD MACHINE

Pod espresso machines can be either semi- or super automatic machines. They are called "pod" machines because they use "pods" of prepared grounds that you throw away after use. There is no grinding or tamping—you buy more pods to make more coffee.

The main downside to a pod machine is you can't adjust the taste of your coffee through blending and adjusting the dosage or fineness of the grounds. You also need to buy their brand of pods (in most cases) so if you can't find one you like, you're out of luck.

STOVETOP MACHINES

For those on a budget who would still like to enjoy a home-brewed cup of espresso, stovetop espresso makers are a good option. The main down-side is these machines can't produce the amount of pressure required for optimal espresso, but that isn't a reason to forego espresso coffee altogether if you don't want to spend more on a machine.

These are very basic devices that are fairly simple to use and care for and require no electricity (this also makes them great for camping!). They are also very popular in Italy, which must say something for the authentic-ity of the results they produce.

If you're wondering which stovetop machines are best, head over to my website at www.makingespresso.com and check out my recommended models.

CHOOSING THE RIGHT MACHINE FOR YOU

While it's generally true that you get what you pay for, machines will out-perform equally priced competitors and some of the more expensive machines actually brew worse coffee than cheaper alternatives.

So, consider the following points of advice when considering which machine to buy.

LOOK AT SEVERAL OPTIONS

Be willing to research several machines before making a final decision. Decide what is the most you want to spend and look at not only machines in that price range, but in lower price ranges too.

LOOK AT REVIEWS

Reading reviews is very important. If you can't find any reliable reviews of a machine, I wouldn't buy it.

To find reviews, I like to use Amazon.com and coffee enthusiast sites like Coffee Geek, Whole Latte Love, and Home-Barista.com.

If you search for reviews of a specific brand or model, watch out for fake review sites set up by Internet marketers that don't know anything about coffee but just want to earn a commission when you click on their link to buy a machine.

FIND A GOOD PRICE AT A GOOD RETAILER

Whether you buy online or off, look around, be sure to check return policies and if you're buying online or from a catalog, make sure you pay attention to the shipping charge before you place your order.

Some sites will offer freebie incentives for buying with them, such as free shipping, free coffee, free machine accessories, and more.

<u>MACHINE FEATURES</u>

The major features will depend on what type of machine you get, and there are a few important points to consider about them. They are as follows:

Metals Used:

All espresso machines heat water in a metal unit of some sort, and the metal(s) used can affect the taste of the espresso. Brass and steel are a better choice than aluminum, which can leave a hint of a metallic taste in your espresso. Aluminum is cheap and lightweight, so it's used in all the low-end models.

Heating System:

Great espresso requires a constant water temperature. Lower-end machines use a thermoblock to heat the water, which is what's used in "instant hot water" taps. Thermoblocks just don't compare to a real boiler in terms of temperature stability. You have to watch out for this one, because some manufacturers have started selling $250+ machines with thermoblocks instead of proper boilers.

Durability:

Watch out for machines with plastic portafilters. These are a definite no-no.

Pump Pressure:

Sometimes manufacturers will make the pressure of a pump seem like it's the most important feature of a machine. This isn't necessarily the case, but it shouldn't be overlooked. The minimum pressure to make espresso is usually considered to be 9 bars, but some people swear by minimums as high as 14 bars. A more powerful pump means a finer grind can be used, increasing the surface area of the coffee and unlocking more of the beans' flavor.

Unless you're buying a very inexpensive stovetop machine, never buy a machine that produces less than 9 bars of pressure.

Steam Wand:

Stovetop machines typically don't include a steam wand, but most others do. Some of the higher-end machines have two boilers—one for the water used to brew the espresso (in which the water doesn't fully boil), and one for creating steam. A double-boiler model doesn't make better coffee than a single-boiler model—it just means you can make cappuccinos and lattes quicker.

Removable Water Reservoir:

The cool thing about these is you can take all the water out of the machine so bacteria won't build up. For health reasons, it's best not to leave water in the machine for extended periods of time.

TIME TO GET A MACHINE!

Hopefully you don't feel overwhelmed by the amount of options and things to consider when buying your machine. If you follow the advice I've given you in this chapter, you'll end up with a good, proven machine that will serve you well.

Once again, if you want to see which brands and models I recommend, I maintain a list of proven winners at <u>www.makingespresso.com</u>.

14

HOW TO KEEP YOUR MACHINE IN TOP-TOP SHAPE

KEEPING YOUR ESPRESSO MACHINE IS an important part of making great coffee and extending the life of your investment. If you don't, rancid oils can build up and ruin your grounds and beverages, and parts can rust and clog.

"Clean" is more than wiping down the drip tray and water spillage, too—it means regularly cleaning internals so they continue to produce the high-quality espresso that you will come to know and love.

DAILY CLEANING ACTIONS

You should purge your steam wand of any remaining liquids and wipe it off after each use.

You should run a water shot through your machine after each brewing session to purge unwanted particles. (Some people even do this after each shot.)

You should use a coffee detergent like Cafiza, JoeGlo, or PuroCaf to rinse, scrub, and wipe the portafilter and basket after each brewing session. Never use a dish detergent on any part of your machine that will come into contact with coffee because these substances are designed to break down oils. Why is that bad? Because a lot of the desirable taste from espresso comes from oils, so you don't want something breaking those oils down.

You should do a clean water back flush every 10 – 15 shots and at the end of each brewing session. (If you don't know what this is, I recommend you do a quick Google search as it requires a couple extra things, and watch a video to see exactly how to do it).

WEEKLY CLEANING ACTIONS

You should do a back flush with a coffee detergent to clean the group head.

You should soak your portafilters and baskets for at least thirty minutes in a solution of coffee detergent and hot water, and scrub, scrub, scrub.

If you can remove the shower screen from the group head, you should take it off along with the dispersion plate, and soak and scrub them just as you do the portafilters.

YEARLY CLEANING ACTIONS

You should descale your espresso machine once per year. This will remove calcium buildup in your boiler tank, which can ruin the taste of your coffee over time and eventually damage your machine.

WOULD YOU DO ME A FAVOR?

THANK YOU FOR BUYING MY book. I hope you have enjoyed it and that it helps you make awesome coffee and save some money.

I have a small favor to ask. Would you mind taking a minute to write a blurb on Amazon about this book? I check all my reviews and love to get feedback (that's the real pay for my work—knowing that I'm helping people make awesome coffee).

Visit the following page to leave me a review:

http://bit.ly/coffeereview

Also, if you have any friends or family that might enjoy this book, spread the love and lend it to them!

And last but not least, my website is www.makingespresso.com, and if you want to write me, my email address is luca@makingespresso.

Thanks again, and I wish you the best!

Luca

Printed in Great Britain
by Amazon.co.uk, Ltd.,
Marston Gate.